Visit the Library's On-line Catalog at:
http://www.zionsville.lib.in.us

Call the Library for information on access
if Internet is not available to you.
(317) 873-3149

On-line magazine index with full text at:
http://www.inspire-indiana.net

P9-DFS-220

OHIO

OHIO

HELLO
U.S.A.

by Dottie Brown

Lerner Publications Company

You'll find this picture of a buckeye tree's leaves at the beginning of each chapter in this book. Ohio's state tree, the buckeye is a type of horse-chestnut tree that is native to North America. The buckeye tree gets its name from its large brown seeds, which resemble the eyes of a buck, or male deer.

Cover (left): The lights of Cinergy Field and the Cincinnati skyline shine on the Ohio River. Cover (right): Rock and Roll Hall of Fame and Museum in Cleveland. Pages 2–3: An Amish farm in Holmes County. Page 3: The Vortex rollercoaster at Paramount's Kings Island in Cincinnati.

This book is available in two editions:
Library binding by Lerner Publications Company, a division of Lerner Publishing Group
Soft cover by First Avenue Editions, an imprint of Lerner Publishing Group
241 First Avenue North
Minneapolis, MN 55401 U.S.A.

Website address: www.lernerbooks.com

Library of Congress Cataloging-in-Publication Data

Brown, Dottie, 1957–
    Ohio / by Dottie Brown—Rev. and expanded 2nd ed.
        p.   cm. — (Hello U.S.A.)
    Includes index.
    ISBN: 0–8225–4075–4 (lib. bdg. : alk. paper)
    ISBN: 0–8225–4134–3 (pbk. : alk. paper)
    1. Ohio—Juvenile literature. [1. Ohio.] I. Title. II. Series.
    F491.3 .B76 2002
    977.1—dc21   2001001739

Manufactured in the United States of America
1 2 3 4 5 6 – JR – 07 06 05 04 03 02

CONTENTS

The Ohio River flows through the city of Cincinnati in southwestern Ohio.

THE LAND

Plains and Plateaus

The state of Ohio takes its name from the wide river that forms its southern and southeastern borders. The Iroquois Indians called this river *oheo*, meaning "beautiful." Another great body of water—Lake Erie, one of the five **Great Lakes**—shapes Ohio's northern border.

Michigan also lies north of Ohio. Pennsylvania and West Virginia border Ohio on the east, Kentucky is to the south, and Indiana is to the west.

More than 20,000 years ago, water in the form of **glaciers** shaped Ohio's land regions. These huge sheets of ice crept over two-thirds of the land that became Ohio, gouging out lake beds and scraping off hilltops. When the glaciers melted, they left behind a thick carpet of **till** (ground-up rocks and dirt).

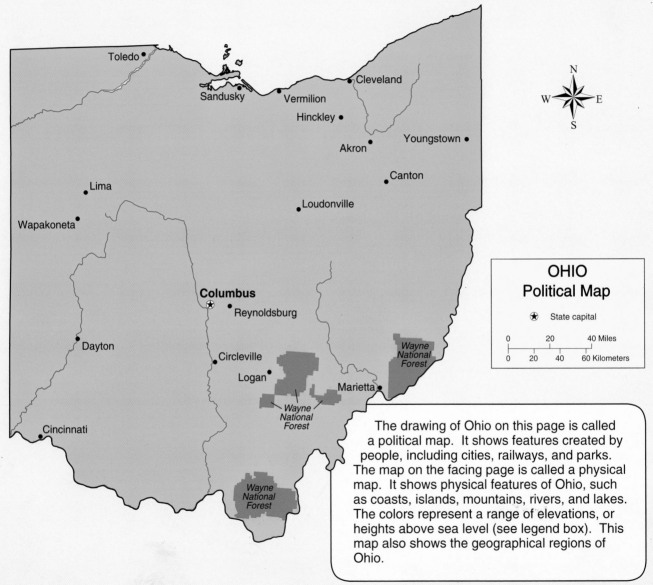

Toledo •

Sandusky
• Vermilion
Hinckley •

• Cleveland

• Youngstown

Akron •

• Canton

Lima •

• Loudonville

Wapakoneta •

Columbus
✪
• Reynoldsburg

Dayton •

• Circleville

Logan •
Marietta •

Wayne National Forest

Cincinnati •

Wayne National Forest

Wayne National Forest

OHIO
Political Map

✪   State capital

0	20	40 Miles
0	20	40 60 Kilometers

The drawing of Ohio on this page is called a political map. It shows features created by people, including cities, railways, and parks. The map on the facing page is called a physical map. It shows physical features of Ohio, such as coasts, islands, mountains, rivers, and lakes. The colors represent a range of elevations, or heights above sea level (see legend box). This map also shows the geographical regions of Ohio.

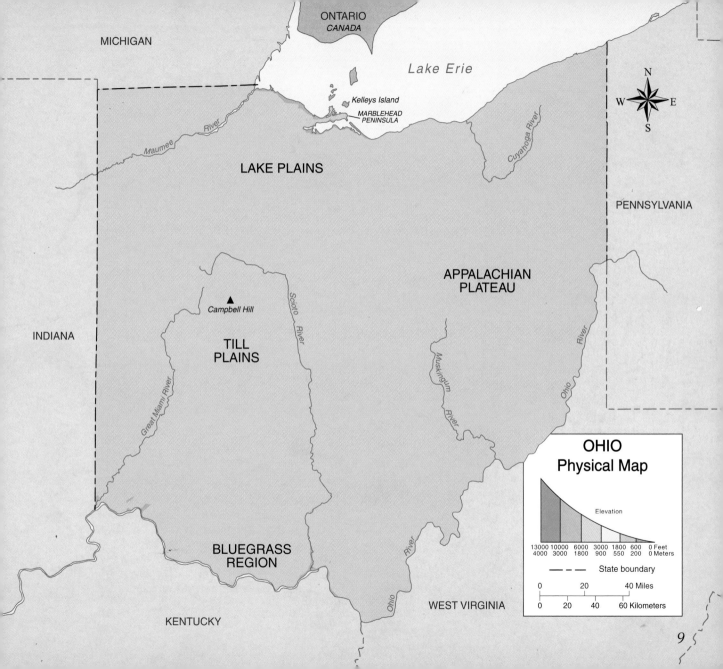

MICHIGAN

ONTARIO
CANADA

Lake Erie

Kelleys Island

MARBLEHEAD
PENINSULA

Cuyahoga River

PENNSYLVANIA

LAKE PLAINS

Maumee River

APPALACHIAN
PLATEAU

▲
Campbell Hill

Scioto River

INDIANA

TILL
PLAINS

Muskingum River

Ohio River

Great Miami River

BLUEGRASS
REGION

Ohio River

WEST VIRGINIA

KENTUCKY

N
W   E
S

OHIO
Physical Map

Elevation

| 13000 | 10000 | 6000 | 3000 | 1800 | 600 | 0 Feet |
| 4000 | 3000 | 1800 | 900 | 550 | 200 | 0 Meters |

– – –   State boundary

| 0 | | 20 | | 40 Miles |

| 0 | 20 | 40 | | 60 Kilometers |

9

One region in Ohio has so much till that it is called the Till Plains. The state's other regions are the Appalachian Plateau, the Bluegrass Region, and the Lake Plains.

The gently rolling Till Plains blanket most of western Ohio. This region contains some of the best farmland in the nation. Low hills stand in the southern Till Plains. One of these, Campbell Hill, is Ohio's highest point.

The Appalachian Plateau covers eastern Ohio. Glaciers moved over only the northern third of the

Visitors stroll under towering cliffs at Hocking Hills State Park in the Appalachian Plateau.

Ohioans fish, boat, and swim at Pike Lake, which is located in the Bluegrass Region.

region, smoothing it out and leaving the fertile soil that is used for farming. Tree-covered hills, deep valleys, and jagged ridges lie south of this farmland. Buried under the **plateau,** or highland, are deposits of coal, oil, clay, and salt.

The Bluegrass Region, a small triangle of land in southern Ohio, is wedged between the Till Plains and the Appalachian Plateau. Flat-topped hills dot the Bluegrass Region.

The Lake Plains region has fertile farmland as well as industrial cities such as Cleveland.

The Lake Plains cut a path across northern Ohio. This region, which holds two of the state's largest cities, borders Lake Erie. A forested swamp once filled the western end of the Lake Plains. In the late 1800s, Ohioans drained the swamp and planted crops there. It is still excellent farmland, as is much of the land in this region.

Lake Erie's shoreline extends 312 miles across northern Ohio. The lake is linked to the Saint Lawrence Seaway, a waterway that connects the Great Lakes to the Atlantic Ocean. The seaway allows Ohioans to ship goods from Lake Erie to markets around the world.

Marblehead Lighthouse, the oldest lighthouse on Lake Erie, brightens the way for ships sailing around Marblehead Peninsula.

An icy stream runs through an Ohio forest in the winter.

The Ohio River has been a valuable water highway for thousands of years. The Great Miami, Scioto, and Muskingum Rivers all flow into the Ohio. Other rivers in Ohio, including the Cuyahoga and the Maumee, travel northward into Lake Erie.

Plenty of rain and snow, about 38 inches a year, feeds Ohio's rivers. Winter temperatures in the state average 28° F. Summer temperatures average 73° F. Tornadoes sometimes twist through Ohio in the spring and fall.

Ohio's warm summers and plentiful rainfall allow many kinds of plants to grow. In the spring, black-eyed Susans, buttercups, and other wildflowers push through the soil. Though settlers cut down many of Ohio's forests to plant crops, large stands of oak, hickory, beech, maple, and sycamore trees still cover about one-fourth of the state.

Ohio's trees turn bright shades of red, yellow, and orange in the fall.

The buckeye—Ohio's state tree—blooms in the springtime.

Ohio's forests are home to many birds, including blackbirds, wrens, and cardinals. The state's large game birds are quail, geese, ducks, and pheasants.

At one time, wolves, bears, buffalo, and deer roamed through Ohio, but few animals of that size remain. The white-tailed deer is the only large animal still thriving in Ohio's countryside. Red foxes, muskrats, woodchucks, opposums, and rabbits also live in the state's forests.

A barn swallow rests on a barbed-wire fence.

Expansion and Industry

 early 13,000 years ago, the first people came to the Ohio area. The ancestors of these ancient Native Americans, or Indians, had probably reached North America by crossing a land bridge that once connected Asia to North America.

The Indians speared beavers as large as bears and huge mastodons—hairy elephants with great tusks. Over time, these large animals disappeared, and the Indians' descendants began to hunt bears and deer. They also gathered berries, nuts, and roots. By about 800 B.C., a group of Indians known as mound builders had replaced the hunters and gatherers.

The Great Serpent Mound is 1,330 feet long and about 4 feet high *(above)*. This skeleton *(left)* was found in an Ohio mound.

The mound builders put their dead in tombs and heaped layers of dirt on the graves, forming mounds of earth. The Indians built other mounds for religious ceremonies. Many of the ceremonial mounds were shaped like animals.

By around A.D. 1600, the mound builders had vanished. No one knows for sure what happened to them. They may have starved when droughts, or long dry spells, caused their crops to fail.

About 100 years later, new groups of Indians moved into the area that later became Ohio. The Shawnee, Miami, and Wyandots were pushed into the area by other nations. People from Great Britain were forming **colonies** (settlements) on the eastern coast of North America, driving the Delaware Indians into Ohio, too.

Fur traders, who began trading with the Indians in the 1700s, paid one dollar for the skin of a male deer, called a buckskin. Buckskin was shortened to buck, which eventually came to mean a dollar bill.

The Indians built their villages along rivers. They fished, gathered wild berries, nuts, and grapes, and planted crops of corn, beans, and tobacco. They also hunted deer, mink, beaver, and fox.

The Indians traded the skins and furs from these animals to the French and British, who had set up trading posts in the region to do business with the Indians. The French and British exchanged kettles, blankets, guns, and other European goods for the furs.

Soon France and Britain each wanted the land and fur trade in North America for themselves. The two countries went to war in 1754. By 1763 the British had gained control of a large area that included Ohio.

But the British did not have this land for long. The colonies wanted to be free from British control, so they went to war with Britain.

When early settlers wanted to clear space for growing crops, they killed trees by making deep slashes in them. The settlers later chopped down the dead trees and burned the trunks.

In 1783 the colonists won the war, called the American Revolution, and formed their own country—the United States of America. In just a few years, settlers had moved into the new country's Northwest Territory, which included the Ohio area. The settlers built Marietta, the first permanent white settlement in Ohio.

As more white settlers came to the territory, the Indians living in the region grew angry. The new-comers were pushing the Indian nations out of the area, just as the colonists had pushed the Delaware out of the East. So the Indians fought to keep their land, attacking settlements.

Settlers arrive at the future site of Cincinnati.

After U.S. troops won the Battle of Fallen Timbers in 1794, pioneers took over most of the land that the Shawnee, Miami, Delaware, and Wyandot Indians had inhabited.

The U.S. government sent soldiers to stop the Indian attacks. Miami chief Little Turtle and his warriors, who came from several nations, won two important battles. But U.S. troops eventually outnumbered and overpowered the Indians.

In 1795 the weakened Indians gave up about two-thirds of the land that became Ohio. Gradually, the U.S. government squeezed the Indians into a small corner of the region, then pushed them out entirely.

No longer fearing Indian attacks, settlers began to pour into the area. Before long, enough people had arrived for the area to qualify for statehood.

The Hinckley Hunt

Farming in the 1800s was hard work. Settlers had to cut crops and carry them to the barn by hand. Storing the harvest was not easy either. Squirrels ate wheat out of barns and stole vegetables from gardens. Deer trampled and ate crops in fields. Wolves killed chickens and sheep. Bears broke into pig pens and ate the pigs.

To get rid of the wild animals, the town of Hinckley, Ohio, held a hunt on Christmas Eve, 1818. More than 500 hunters encircled the town. Then they moved inward, killing every animal in sight. At the end of the day, the hunters divided up the bounty and took it home to eat.

Sailors push a keelboat up the Ohio River.

On March 1, 1803, Ohio was carved out of the Northwest Territory and became the 17th state.

About 70,000 Ohioans lived in the new state. Many were farmers who needed to get their crops and livestock to market quickly. But the few roads that existed were rough and took weeks to travel. Crops could easily spoil before they reached their destination—if they got there at all.

Ohioans used rivers as highways to transport their goods. Because it flows through many states, the Ohio River was an especially important trade route.

At first, keelboats carried the crops to their destination. Keelboats were long boats with sails.

Cargo from canal boats was put on steamboats like this one, which carried the goods to market.

The river current took the keelboat downriver quickly, but the boat's crew had to push the boat all the way back upriver using long poles.

In 1811 steamboats appeared on the Ohio River. With their steam-powered paddles and large storage spaces, steamboats could carry more crops faster than keelboats. By 1825 barges had begun to travel the Erie Canal. This humanmade waterway was built to connect Lake Erie to the Hudson River in New York. Ohio's farmers now had a direct water route to the large markets of New York City.

Ohio's population soon swelled to nearly 1.5 million. In 1839 the state led the nation in wheat production. By 1850 Ohio ranked first in horse and sheep population. Hog and dairy farming became important, too. Workers in Cincinnati slaughtered and packed so many hogs—more than 400,000 a year—that the city was called Porkopolis.

Ohio's natural resources helped industry develop rapidly in the state. For example, the state's strong river currents powered mills, which ground farmers' corn and wheat into meal and flour.

About 1,500 hogs were butchered and cleaned in Cincinnati's meat-packing plants every day.

During the mid-1800s, some Ohioans worked at pottery factories that sprang up near clay deposits in eastern and south central Ohio.

Woodworkers crafted furniture, barrels, and wagons from Ohio's trees. Potters made dishes and jugs out of clay found in the state. Miners chiseled tons of coal out of the earth to power steam engines.

Ohio's industries created jobs that drew thousands of people to the state, including slaves who had escaped from the South, where slavery was legal. When the U.S. government passed laws making it hard for former slaves to remain safely in Ohio, many Ohioans helped the runaways flee to Canada, where slave owners could not legally chase them. The system that helped escaped slaves reach a safe place was called the **Underground Railroad**.

The Ohioans who ran the Underground Railroad, as well as many Americans in other states, wanted to outlaw slavery in every state. In 1861 several Southern states withdrew from the Union to form a separate country where slavery would remain legal.

The Underground Railroad

In 1852 Harriet Beecher Stowe wrote *Uncle Tom's Cabin*. This book described the cruelty of slavery and the desperate attempts slaves made to escape. Stowe based the book on true stories she had heard from escaped slaves while she lived in Cincinnati. Stowe's powerful book, which sold millions of copies, helped convince many people that slavery was wrong.

Some Ohioans who agreed with Stowe were part of the Underground Railroad. They hid escaped slaves in wagons, canal boats, trains, barns, and homes. The slaves usually traveled at night to avoid being caught. If they were captured and returned to their owners, slaves would not only lose their freedom, they were also likely to be severely punished. People who helped escaped slaves risked going to jail.

To keep the Union together, the North fought against the South in what became known as the Civil War. Nearly 350,000 Ohioans helped the North win the war by 1865.

After the war, Ohio's industries continued to grow. Railroads were one reason for this success. Ohio farmers and merchants could send their goods

Oil produced in western Ohio was carried by railroad to Cleveland.

Oil was cleaned in Cleveland's factories before it was sent on to other states.

quickly by railroad all across the country. Thousands of miles of railroad tracks stretched through Ohio.

Natural resources, especially coal, oil, and natural gas, also continued to be a key to Ohio's industrial success. Most factories and railroads depended on these fuels to power their machinery. Because Ohio had plenty of cheap fuel, industries from all over the country were drawn to the state.

One of these was the rubber industry. In 1870 Benjamin F. Goodrich moved his rubber factory from New York to Akron. At first the factory made fire hoses, but it later produced tires for the cars and trucks made in Ohio and in nearby Michigan.

Steel was another important industry. Ships on Lake Erie brought iron ore to Ohio, where the metal was used to make steel. The state's steel industry has grown to be the second largest in the country.

Ohio inventors created even more industries. In 1903 Wilbur and Orville Wright, bicycle mechanics from Dayton, Ohio, made the first successful flight in an airplane. Their work encouraged other people around the world to design and build more aircraft.

When the United States entered World War I in 1917, all of Ohio's industries became even busier. Workers made rubber, airplanes, and parts for cars and trucks, all of which were needed to fight the war. When the war ended, however, so did the high demand for Ohio's products. Factories closed, and in Akron alone, 50,000 people lost their jobs.

The Day Dayton Drowned

Before dams were built to control flooding, Ohioans expected floods. The Ohio River spilled over its banks almost every spring. During the winter, blocks of ice often backed up the state's northern rivers, causing more flooding. But the flood of 1913 was Ohio's worst. Three days of pouring rain swelled rivers to overflowing. Almost every Ohio city near a river was flooded, and nearly 500 people were killed. Dayton was hardest hit. Twenty feet of water covered its downtown area, and businesses lost hundreds of millions of dollars in property damage.

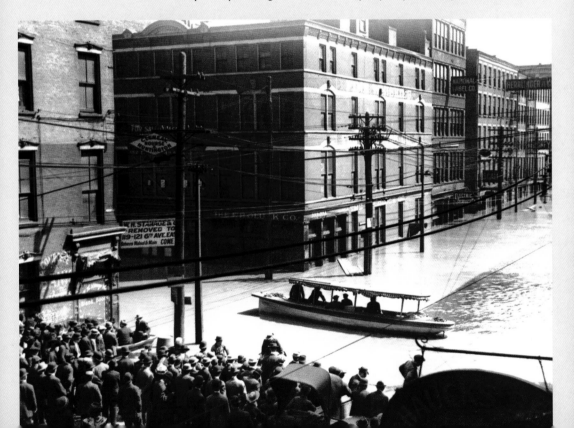

During the Great Depression, nearly half of Ohio's factory workers lost their jobs. The government tried to help them by giving them money to live on. Here, unemployed Clevelanders line up to collect government aid.

Then the Great Depression, a time when many banks and businesses shut down, hit the country in 1929. The depression, which lasted through the 1930s, left many Americans without jobs or money. More factories closed and many of Ohio's farmers lost their land.

Ohio's industries started up again in 1941, when the United States entered World War II. Workers again built ships, airplanes, and weapons. Farmers

During World War II, many women worked in factories making bombs, torpedoes, trucks, and tanks.

grew tons of grain to feed the soldiers fighting overseas. A company in Toledo made jeeps for the troops, while other factories made huge tanks.

After the war ended in 1945, Ohio continued to prosper. The state's population grew, and almost everyone who needed to earn money could find a job.

Not everyone prospered in Ohio's healthy economy. In the 1950s and 1960s, many Ohioans who lived in cities were very poor. A large number of these people were black. They wanted better jobs, better housing, and the same rights as white people.

During this time, African American people all over the country were working together to fight for equal rights. Unfortunately, the struggle sometimes turned violent. In 1966 racial tension led to rioting in Cleveland.

Also around this time, the United States became involved in the Vietnam War. Many Americans protested against the war. At an anti-war protest at Kent State University near Akron in 1970, four students were killed and several were wounded by members of the National Guard.

On May 4, 1970, National Guardsmen fired into a crowd of protestors at Kent State University in Ohio. Four students were killed.

In the 1980s, Clevelanders spent millions of dollars to rebuild their downtown.

By the end of the 1970s, some of Ohio's industries had moved to states where the costs of running a business were lower. These industries took thousands of jobs with them.

The 1970s and 1980s were hard for Ohio, but the state has learned from its difficulties. Ohioans are working in many ways—lowering taxes, building new office buildings, and making new highways—to keep the state's industries strong.

During the 1990s, businesses began to prosper again, and new businesses were attracted to the state. Public schools were improved, and Ohioans decided to spend money to upgrade their state's parks. Ohio looks to the future with hope for its economy, its children, and its natural areas.

PEOPLE & ECONOMY

The Heart of It All

When it comes to people, Ohio is a giant. With more than 11 million residents, Ohio ranks seventh in population in the United States. But the state is not large in terms of land— 34 states are larger.

About three-fourths of all Ohioans live in cities. The state's largest cities are Columbus (the capital), Cleveland, and Cincinnati. Ohio has six cities with populations over 150,000.

Almost all Ohioans were born in the United States, but their ancestors came from around the world. Many sailed from Great Britain. Others came later from Germany, Italy, Poland, Greece, Hungary, and elsewhere in Europe.

Columbus—Ohio's capital city—was built along the Scioto River.

Ohioans celebrate their German heritage at Oktoberfest.

A little more than 11 percent of Ohio's people are African American. Hispanics, Native Americans, and Asians together make up only about 3 percent of the state's population.

Ohioans are proud of their educational system. Oberlin College was the first in the nation to educate men and women together. And Wilberforce University was the first U.S. college for African American students.

Airplane fans in Ohio can see World War II bombers, as well as an Apollo space capsule, at the huge U.S. Air Force Museum near Dayton. History buffs can visit Roscoe Village, a town on the Ohio and Erie Canal rebuilt to look like it did in the middle of the 1800s. As visitors walk alongside Serpent Mound in southwestern Ohio, they can imagine what Ohio was like in the days of the mound builders.

Sports enthusiasts will find plenty to watch in Ohio. Two professional baseball teams play in the state—the Cincinnati Reds and the Cleveland Indians. Ohio is also home to two pro football teams, the Cincinnati Bengals and the Cleveland Browns. The state also has two basketball teams—the Cleveland Cavaliers and the Cleveland Rockers, a professional women's team.

A Cleveland Indian at work

Riders on the Witches' Wheel at Cedar Point in Sandusky, Ohio, whirl high above the ground.

For people who prefer doing to watching, Ohio offers lots of choices. Canoeists can glide down the hundreds of miles of rivers and creeks in the state. The Wayne National Forest, which covers a large part of southeastern Ohio, has wilderness trails for those who want to hike. Thrill seekers can ride the roller coasters at popular amusement parks such as Kings

Island near Cincinnati and Cedar Point in Sandusky.

Service jobs employ about two-thirds of workers in Ohio. People who work for restaurants, shops, hospitals, hotels, and banks have service jobs. Many service workers in Ohio also sell and trade items such as food, coal, cars, and steel.

Some service workers, like this Lake Erie ferryboat captain, go to work on Ohio's lakes and rivers.

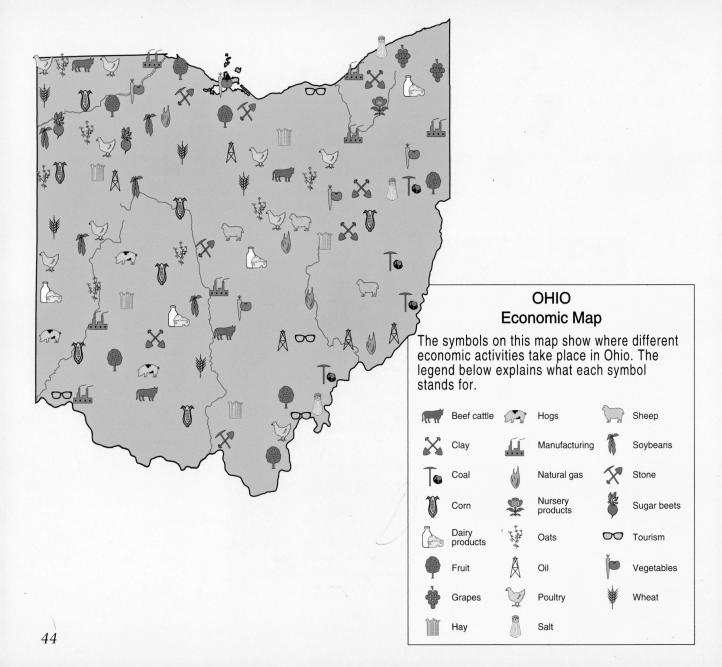

OHIO
Economic Map

The symbols on this map show where different economic activities take place in Ohio. The legend below explains what each symbol stands for.

	Beef cattle		Hogs		Sheep
	Clay		Manufacturing		Soybeans
	Coal		Natural gas		Stone
	Corn		Nursery products		Sugar beets
	Dairy products		Oats		Tourism
	Fruit		Oil		Vegetables
	Grapes		Poultry		Wheat
	Hay		Salt		

Other service workers move Ohio's products into and out of the state by ship, river barge, railroad, airplane, or truck. Almost 60 percent of the money earned in Ohio comes from services.

About one-sixth of Ohio's workers manufacture products. Workers at metal foundries make steel.

A worker puts an airplane engine together at a factory.

Ohio's steel is sold across the nation. Within Ohio, some of the steel is used to mold parts for cars, trucks, airplanes, washing machines, and air conditioners. Many Ohio workers assemble cars and trucks. Rubber companies make tires in Akron, Cleveland, and Dayton. The largest soap factory in the United States is in Cincinnati.

Ohioans also prepare lots of different foods. In Cincinnati, workers pack meat. In Columbus,

Ohioans put together cars on an assembly line.

Many apple trees grow in Ohio. During the 1800s, Johnny Appleseed planted thousands of apple seeds there.

workers brew beer and bake breads and pastries. Tuscarawas, a county in eastern Ohio, makes so much Swiss cheese that the area has been nicknamed Little Switzerland.

Only a small number of Ohioans farm for a living. Farmers make just 1 percent of the money earned in Ohio. The two main crops are corn and soybeans. Farmers also grow large crops of cucumbers, tomatoes, and wheat.

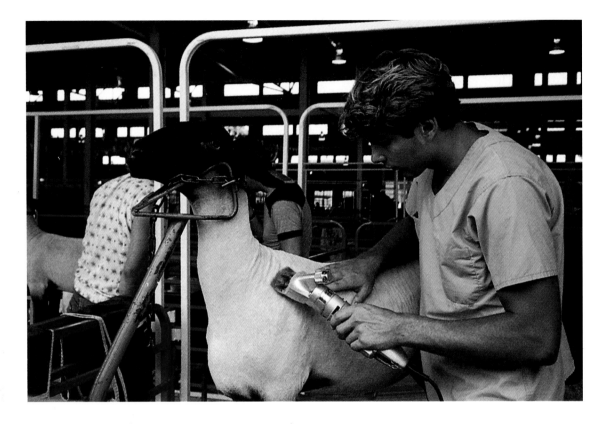

A sheep farmer shears, or shaves off, a sheep's wool.

Warm breezes from Lake Erie help protect fruit crops in northern Ohio from frost in spring and fall. As a result, many farmers are able to grow grapes and strawberries.

Ohio is a leading producer of hogs. Many farmers in southwestern Ohio raise hogs, which are sold to meat-packing plants in Cincinnati. There they are butchered and packaged to be sold in supermarkets. Dairy cattle graze on farms in southeastern Ohio. Livestock farmers in other areas of the state raise sheep and poultry.

Very few Ohioans are miners. But these few people remove millions of tons of coal from the earth every year. Other miners dig for salt and limestone, drill for petroleum and natural gas, and cut sandstone.

Miners extract limestone from central Ohio. Some of the limestone goes into cement, which is used to construct roads, sidewalks, and buildings.

Ohio's fertile farmland, mineral supplies, industries, and shipping ports provide many different kinds of work for Ohioans. The food and goods that these workers produce are used not only by other Ohioans but also by many people across the nation.

A cargo ship on the Ohio River

THE ENVIRONMENT

Troubled Land and Waters

hio's land has always provided food, shelter, and jobs for residents of the state. Rivers and streams supply water for crops growing in the rich soil. Trees furnish wood for homes, furniture, and ships. The earth holds fuels such as coal and gas.

These natural resources have helped Ohio grow. Although the state is small, it has more industries than most other states its size. But the more Ohio's industries produce, the more they pollute the land. In fact, Ohio's industries have grown so much that they are poisoning the natural resources on which they depend.

Ohio's industries are important to its economy, but they also pollute the environment.

Most industries produce waste materials that hold pollutants. Some of the waste is toxic, or poisonous. Over the years, Ohio's many industries have formed hundreds of millions of tons of **toxic waste**. In 1996 alone, 115 million pounds of toxic waste were produced in Ohio. Much of this waste goes into dumps or into **landfills,** places where trash is buried.

Individuals have added to the problem, especially since the state's population has grown to more than 11 million residents. People create more toxic waste when they throw away items such as paint, paint remover, and bug spray.

Landfills and dumps where toxic waste is found are called **hazardous waste sites.** Hazardous waste sites are dangerous because they produce toxic **leachate.** Leachate is rainwater that falls on toxic waste in landfills or dumps and absorbs the poisons that are in the waste.

If toxic leachate seeps into the ground, it can kill plants. It can also poison the **groundwater**— clean water beneath the ground that is used for drinking water by over one-fourth of all Ohioans.

Some of the toxic leachate washes into rivers and streams, poisoning or killing fish and other wildlife. Studies have shown that people who drink toxic water or eat poisoned fish may have a higher risk of developing cancer or other illnesses.

Ohio ranks 10th in the nation in the number of hazardous waste sites controlled by the federal government. In 1998 the federal government was in charge of 36 hazardous waste sites in Ohio, and there were hundreds more. Many of these sites are very likely to leak toxic waste or leachate.

Ohioans are working to clean up these sites. Ohio is asking its citizens to reduce toxic waste by using fewer poisonous products.

A sign warns of the dangers of hazardous waste.

Sometimes chemicals and other wastes leak from barrels at hazardous waste sites, polluting the ground and the water.

People can also help by bringing poisonous wastes to hazardous waste centers rather than throwing the materials into the trash.

The state government has set up strict laws regarding toxic waste in landfills. If industries put their toxic wastes into landfills, the landfills must be built specifically to hold toxic waste. New landfills must have machines that collect and clean leachate.

Nail polish, oven cleaner, batteries, and other hazardous wastes are often dumped into landfills along with other garbage.

The landfills must also be lined with clay and plastic to keep leachate from seeping into the ground.

Not all Ohioans welcome these laws, which make getting rid of toxic waste more difficult. The sealed landfills that meet new regulations are more expensive to operate than the old landfills. When businesses decide that Ohio's toxic waste laws cost too much to follow, the companies sometimes move to states that have weaker laws. Ohio then loses jobs and money.

Ohioans must decide whether careless waste disposal is more harmful than unemployment. The

Cuyahoga River is a reminder of how harmful toxic waste can be. The river was once so filled with oil and toxic wastes that fish and other wildlife could not live in it. In 1969 the Cuyahoga River actually caught on fire.

The fire forced industries and individuals to start disposing of toxic wastes in safer, smarter ways.

Paint collection programs can help keep landfills free of hazardous waste.

Pollution still flows into Ohio waterways in some places.

The federal government passed the Clean Water Act in 1972, which stopped much of the toxic waste dumping. In addition, Ohio has spent more than $1.5 billion to create better sewage treatment plants.

The Cuyahoga has gotten much cleaner since the late 1960s. Fish and birds have returned to the river, and Ohioans spend time in parks near the river. However, wastes from factories and from hazardous waste sites still pollute the river. It is unsafe to eat fish from the river or to swim in most places along the river. The Cuyahoga will not be completely healthy for many years.

The Cuyahoga River fire showed Ohioans that if industries and residents don't take care of toxic waste, Ohio becomes an unhealthy place to live and work. To prevent this from happening, many Ohioans are striving to make their state cleaner and safer for generations to come.

Students test a stream for pollution.

Fun Facts

Every year on March 15, a flock of buzzards heading north for the summer flies into Hinckley, Ohio. The people of Hinckley celebrate the arrival of the birds with a festival on Buzzard Day, the first Sunday after March 15.

In 1869 the Cincinnati Red Stockings became the first professional baseball team in the United States.

John Glenn, the first American to orbit the earth in a spaceship, and Neil Armstrong, the first person to walk on the moon, were both born in Ohio.

Buzzard

Ohio is known as the Mother of Presidents. Seven U.S. presidents—Ulysses S. Grant, Rutherford B. Hayes, James Garfield, Benjamin Harrison, William McKinley, William Howard Taft, and Warren Harding—came from Ohio.

Ohio produces more tomatoes than any state except California. In fact, the city of Reynoldsburg, Ohio, is known as the Birthplace of the Tomato.

Between 1870 and the mid-1900s, more rubber tires were made in Akron, Ohio, than in any other place in the world. The city was known as the Rubber Capital of the World.

The city of Cleveland, Ohio, got its name from its founder, General Moses Cleaveland. The spelling changed in 1832, when a newspaper, *The Cleaveland Advertiser*, couldn't fit its name across the front page.

During the mid-1800s, when Cincinnati was home to many pig farms and pork packagers, pigs freely roamed the streets. For six months during 2000, hundreds of pigs were again at home in the streets of Cincinnati. This time they were sculptures created to recognize the city's history.

STATE SONG

"Beautiful Ohio" was written in 1918 and adopted as Ohio's official state song in 1969.
In 1989 new words for the song were written and officially adopted.

BEAUTIFUL OHIO

Music by Mary Earl
Words by Wilbert B. McBride

Beau - ti - ful O - hi - o, where the gold - en grain Dwarf the love - ly

flow - ers in the sum - mer rain. Cit - ies ris - ing

high, _____ Sil - hou - ette the sky. _____

Free - dom is su - preme in this ma - jes - tic land; Might - y fac - t'ries

seem to hum a tune so grand. Beau - ti - ful O - hi - o, thy

won - ders are in view, Land where my dreams all come true. _____

You can hear "Beautiful Ohio" by visiting this website:

<http://www.50states.com/songs/ohio.htm>

62

AN OHIO RECIPE

The buckeye tree—Ohio's state tree—provides cool shade and grows beautiful white blossoms. The trees have seeds that grow inside leathery cases protected by spikes. The seed itself is shiny and brown. It is called a buckeye because it looks like the eye of a buck, or male deer. With the recipe below, you can make a tasty treat that looks like a buckeye seed.

BUCKEYE TREATS

Ask an adult for help with using the oven.

1 ½ cups peanut butter
6 cups confectioners' sugar
1 cup butter, softened

½ teaspoon vanilla extract
4 cups semisweet chocolate chips

1. Combine peanut butter, sugar, butter and vanilla extract. Dough will look dry.
2. Roll dough into balls about 1 inch in diameter and place on cookie sheet lined with wax paper.
3. Insert toothpick into each ball (to be used as handle during dipping) and chill in freezer until hard (about ½ hour).
4. Melt chocolate chips. Use top of double boiler over very low heat for best results (otherwise chocolate gets grainy texture).
5. Dip frozen dough balls in the chocolate using toothpick as handle. Leave small circle of dough uncovered to make it look like buckeye.
6. Place buckeyes back on cookie sheet and refrigerate for 2 hours.

HISTORICAL TIMELINE

11,000 B.C. The first people enter the area that later became Ohio.

800 B.C. Mound builders in the Ohio area make villages and mounds.

A.D. 1600 Mound builders disappear from the Ohio area.

1763 The British gain control of the land that includes Ohio.

1788 Marietta, Ohio's first white settlement, is built.

1795 Indians are forced to give most of Ohio to the U.S. government.

1803 Ohio becomes the 17th state.

1811 The first steamboat travels the Ohio River.

1839 Ohio leads the nation in wheat production.

1850 Ohio is a leading producer and packager of hogs, and Cincinnati is nicknamed Porkopolis.

1852 Harriet Beecher Stowe, who lived in Cincinnati, writes *Uncle Tom's Cabin*.

1870 Benjamin Goodrich starts Ohio's first rubber factory.

1913 Ohio's largest recorded flood hits the state.

1917 Ohio's factories begin producing materials to help the United States fight World War I.

1941 Thousands of women take jobs in Ohio's factories as the United States enters World War II.

1966 Racial tension leads to riots in Cleveland.

1969 The Cuyahoga River catches fire in Cleveland.

1970 Four student antiwar protestors are killed by members of the National Guard at Kent State University near Akron.

1980 Cleveland begins to rebuild its downtown.

1993 Ohioans vote to spend $200 million to improve their state's parks and recreation areas.

2001 Riots break out in Cincinnati, following the shooting of an African American man by police.

Daniel Beard

Paul Laurence Dunbar

Thomas Alva Edison

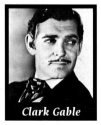

Clark Gable

OUTSTANDING OHIOANS

Neil Armstrong (born 1930), an astronaut, is from Wapakoneta. On July 20, 1969, Armstrong was the first person to walk on the moon. As he stepped onto the moon's surface, he made the famous comment, "That's one small step for a man, one giant leap for mankind."

Daniel Beard (1850–1941), of Cincinnati, was a writer and outdoorsman. His boys' club, the Sons of Daniel Boone, merged with a British group to become the Boy Scouts of America. He led the Boy Scouts for 31 years.

Paul Laurence Dunbar (1872–1906) was one of the first widely known black writers and one of the most popular American poets of his time. His books include *Lyrics of Lowly Life* and *The Sport of the Gods.* He was born in Dayton, Ohio.

Thomas Alva Edison (1847–1931) was one of the world's greatest inventors. He created the electric light bulb, the phonograph, the movie camera, and many other things. He held more U.S. patents than anyone in history. Edison was born in Milan, Ohio.

Harvey Firestone (1868–1938) started the Firestone Tire & Rubber Company in 1900. A native of Columbiana, Ohio, Firestone built his tire business in Akron. His company grew to be one of the largest rubber tire producers in the world.

Clark Gable (1901–1960), born in Cadiz, Ohio, was an actor who starred in more than 70 films. Gable is probably best known for playing the role of Rhett Butler in *Gone with the Wind.*

John Glenn (born 1921) is an astronaut and politician from Cambridge, Ohio. In 1962 he became the first American to orbit the earth. He served as a U.S. senator from Ohio from 1975 until 1998. In 1998 he returned to space. At age 77, he was the oldest person ever to travel in space.

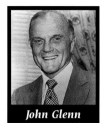

John Glenn

Virginia Hamilton (born 1936) is an award-winning author of fiction and nonfiction for children. Her books include *The House of Dies Drear*, *The Planet of Junior Brown*, and *Sweet Whispers, Brother Rush*. She was the first African American woman to win a Newbery Award, an honor she received for *M.C. Higgins, the Great*. Hamilton lives in her Ohio hometown, Yellow Springs.

Maya Lin (born 1959) is a sculptor and architect who designed the Vietnam Veterans' Memorial in Washington, D.C., and the Civil Rights Memorial in Montgomery, Alabama. Lin is a native of Athens, Ohio.

Maya Lin

Toni Morrison (born 1931), from Lorain, Ohio, has written several books, including *The Bluest Eye*, *Song of Solomon*, and *Jazz*. She won a Pulitzer Prize in 1988 for her novel *Beloved*. In 1993 Morrison became the first African American to win the Nobel Prize for literature.

Toni Morrison

Annie Oakley (1860–1926) was an expert gunslinger who became famous for her performances with Buffalo Bill's Wild West Show. Born in Darke County, Ohio, Oakley was so skilled with a gun that she could blast a cigarette out of a person's mouth without even scratching the person.

Annie Oakley

Ransom Eli Olds (1864–1950), of Geneva, Ohio, was an inventor and manufacturer of automobiles. He founded Olds Motor Works in 1899. The company built the first Oldsmobile two years later.

Jesse Owens

Jesse Owens (1913–1980) moved to Cleveland at the age of seven. A star in track and field at Ohio State University, Owens won four gold medals at the 1936 Summer Olympic Games in Berlin, Germany. During his career, he broke seven world records.

Pontiac (1720–1769), an Ottawa Indian chief, united the Indian nations of the Great Lakes region to fight white settlers. In 1763 Pontiac and his warriors attacked British forts and settlements in what became known as Pontiac's War. He was born in northern Ohio.

Branch Rickey

Branch Rickey (1881–1965) grew up near Toledo. Rickey was a baseball catcher, coach, manager, and executive. He signed on Jackie Robinson, the first African American to play baseball in the modern major leagues.

Pete Rose (born 1941) played baseball for his hometown team, the Cincinnati Reds, and later became the team's manager. Rose is the all-time leading hitter in major-league baseball, with 4,256 hits. He was banned from baseball for gambling, or betting money, on the game.

Pete Rose

Steven Spielberg (born 1947) is a screenwriter, director, and producer who was born in Cincinnati. His many successful movies include *E.T.: The Extra-Terrestrial*, *Raiders of the Lost Ark*, *Schindler's List*, and *Jurassic Park*.

Steven Spielberg

Gloria Steinem (born 1934) is a writer and activist from Toledo. Since the 1960s, Steinem has worked for women's rights, civil rights, and global peace. She cofounded the magazines *New York* and *Ms.* and has written several books.

Gloria Steinem

Tecumseh (1768–1813) was a Shawnee chief from Old Piqua, Ohio, who worked to unite the Indians of the Ohio Valley. He encouraged tribespeople to fight to keep white settlers from taking the Indians' land. Tecumseh helped the British fight against American settlers in the War of 1812.

Tecumseh

James Thurber (1894–1961) was an author and cartoonist who was born in Columbus. His classic short story "The Secret Life of Walter Mitty" depicts an anxious man who finds relief in daydreams. Many of his stories and cartoons were published in *The New Yorker* magazine.

Ted Turner (born 1938) is a highly successful broadcasting executive who was born in Cincinnati. He created the Cable News Network (CNN), the first 24-hour news channel. His empire has included several television networks and several sports teams. In 1997 he donated $1 billion to the United Nations.

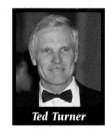

Ted Turner

Orville Wright (1871–1948) was an inventor born in Dayton. In 1903 at Kitty Hawk, North Carolina, along with his brother Wilbur, he made the first successful airplane flight.

Cy Young (1867–1955), of Gilmore, Ohio, was one of baseball's greatest pitchers. During his 21-year career in the major leagues he won a record 511 games. Young was elected to the Baseball Hall of Fame in 1937.

Orville Wright

FACTS-AT-A-GLANCE

Nickname: Buckeye State

Song: "Beautiful Ohio"

Motto: With God All Things Are Possible

Flower: red carnation

Tree: buckeye

Bird: cardinal

Animal: white-tailed deer

Insect: ladybug

Fossil: trilobite

Gemstone: flint

Date and ranking of statehood: March 1, 1803, the 17th state

Capital: Columbus

Area: 40,953 square miles

Rank in area, nationwide: 35th

Average January temperature: 28°F

Average July temperature: 73°F

Ohio's flag is the only state flag in the country that is shaped like a swallow's tail. The blue triangle represents the state's hills and valleys The white circle is an "O" for "Ohio."

POPULATION GROWTH

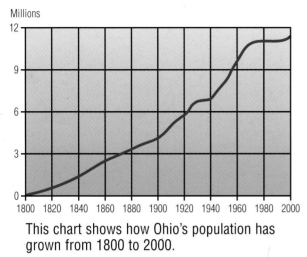

This chart shows how Ohio's population has grown from 1800 to 2000.

Population: 11,353,140 (2000 census)

Rank in population, nationwide: 7th

Major cities and populations: (2000 census) Columbus (711,470), Cleveland (478,403), Cincinnati (331,285), Toledo (313,619), Akron (217,074)

U.S. senators: 2

U.S. representatives: 18

Electoral votes: 20

Natural resources: clay, coal, fertile soil, limestone, natural gas, oil, salt, sandstone

Agricultural products: apples, beef cattle, corn, cucumbers, grapes, hogs, milk, poultry, soybeans, tomatoes

Manufactured goods: aircraft parts, cars, chemicals, clay, construction machinery, glass, ovens, rubber, steel, trucks, washing machines

Ohio's state seal was adopted in 1967. It shows a bundle of 17 arrows, because Ohio was the 17th state. Fields and wheat, representing agriculture in Ohio, also appear on the seal. To show that Ohio was the first state west of the Allegheny Mountains, the sun rises over mountains and the Scioto River.

WHERE OHIOANS WORK

Services—64 percent (services includes jobs in trade; community, social, and personal services; finance, insurance, and real estate; transportation, communication, and utilities)

Manufacturing—17 percent

Government—12 percent

Construction—5 percent

Agriculture—2 percent

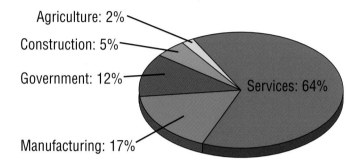

Agriculture: 2%
Construction: 5%
Government: 12%
Services: 64%
Manufacturing: 17%

GROSS STATE PRODUCT

Services—59 percent

Manufacturing—26 percent

Government—10 percent

Construction—4 percent

Agriculture—1 percent

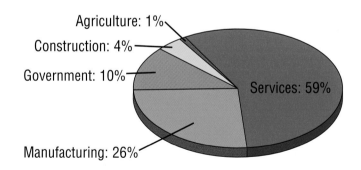

Agriculture: 1%
Construction: 4%
Government: 10%
Services: 59%
Manufacturing: 26%

STATE WILDLIFE

Mammals: beaver, mink, muskrat, opossum, rabbit, raccoon, red fox, skunk, squirrel, white-tailed deer, woodchuck

Birds: bald eagle, blackbird, brown thrasher, cardinal, chickadee, duck, goose, meadowlark, pheasant, quail, robin, ruffed grouse, sparrow, swallow, turkey, wren

Amphibians and reptiles: copperhead snakes, freshwater mussels, swamp rattlesnakes, timber rattlesnakes, treefrogs

Fish: bass, bluegill, catfish, muskellunge, perch, pike, walleye

Trees: beech, black walnut, hickory, maple, pine, red and white oak, sycamore, tulip tree, white ash, white elm

Wild plants: anemone, blazing star, blue sage, Indian pipe, lily, saxifrage, toothwort, wild indigo

Beavers live in Ohio's forests.

PLACES TO VISIT

Amish Country, Holmes County

The largest Amish population in North America lives in this part of northeastern Ohio. Visitors can explore one of the Amish farms that are open to the public and buy homemade wares from craftspeople.

Cedar Point, Sandusky

Daredevils have been heading to this amusement park since 1870. It has 68 rides, including 14 roller coasters. It also boasts the tallest, fastest roller coaster in the world, the Millennium Force.

Hocking Hills State Park, near Logan

Hikers, rock climbers, canoeists, and bikers enjoy exploring this park. The popular hills feature caves, unusual rock formations, and waterfalls.

Kelleys Island, Lake Erie

The largest American island in Lake Erie features spectacular rock formations, including those shaped by glaciers at the Glacial Grooves State Memorial. Native Americans drew plants and animals on the rocks at Inscription Rock State Memorial.

Neil Armstrong Air & Space Museum, Wapakoneta

Located in the pioneering astronaut's hometown, this museum displays planes, rockets and other artifacts that document the history of space travel.

Pro Football Hall of Fame, Canton
This museum explores the history of the National Football League and honors its stars through multimedia exhibits.

Roscoe Village, Coshocton County
Situated on the Erie Canal, this re-creation of a mid-1800s village features a blacksmith shop, a canal tollhouse, a school, a restaurant, and other buildings. Visitors can take a ride on a horse-drawn canal boat.

Serpent Mound, Adams County
This 2,000-year-old mound in the shape of a snake is a quarter of a mile long. Visitors can look at the mound and visit a museum that displays artifacts found in the area.

U.S. Air Force Museum, Fairborn
Located near Dayton, the largest air and space museum in the world displays 300 planes and missiles. In the hometown of the Wright brothers, visitors can learn about the history of flight, from hot air balloons to bombers.

Wayne National Forest
This park, located in the foothills of the Appalachian Mountains, covers three major areas in southeastern Ohio. There are trails for hiking and many other opportunities for nature lovers.

A waterfall in Hocking Hills State Park

ANNUAL EVENTS

Buzzard Day, Hinckley—*March*

Festival of the Fish, Vermilion—*June*

Dayton Air Show, Fairborn—*July*

Great Mohican Indian Powwow, Loudonville—*July*

Pro Football Hall of Fame Festival, Canton—*July*

Soap Box Derby, Akron—*August*

The Reynoldsburg Tomato Festival, Reynoldsburg—*September*

Pumpkin Show, Circleville—*October*

First Night, Akron—*December*

LEARN MORE ABOUT OHIO

BOOKS

General

Fradin, Dennis Brindell. *Ohio.* Chicago: Children's Press, 1993.

Heinrichs, Ann. *Ohio.* Danbury, CT: Children's Press, 1999. For older readers.

Wills, Charles A. *A Historical Album of Ohio.* Brookfield, CT: The Millbrook Press, 1996.

Special Interest

Cwiklik, Robert. *Tecumseh: Shawnee Rebel.* Broomall, PA: Chelsea House, 1994. Tells the story of Tecumseh's struggle to unite the Indian nations in the Ohio area and defend against advancing white settlers.

Fradin, Dennis Brindell. *Bound for the North Star: True Stories of Fugitive Slaves.* New York: Clarion Books, 2000. A collection of true stories of slaves who escaped and people who helped them along the Underground Railroad.

Kramer, Barbara. *John Glenn: A Space Biography.* Springfield, NJ: Enslow Publishers, Inc., 1998. Describes the life of this astronaut and senator from Ohio, from his childhood up to his 1998 flight as the oldest person ever in space.

Sutcliffe, Jane. *Jesse Owens.* Minneapolis: Carolrhoda Books, Inc., 2001. This colorfully illustrated book describes Jesse Owens's childhood, his track career in Ohio, and his experience at the 1936 Olympic Games in Berlin.

Fiction

Durrant, Lynda. *The Beaded Moccasins: The Story of Mary Campbell.* New York: Clarion Books, 1998. Based on a true story, this historical novel describes the experiences of Mary Campbell, a 12-year-old girl who was kidnapped from her home in Pennsylvania by Delaware Indians and taken to their home in Ohio.

Hamilton, Virginia. *M.C. Higgins, the Great.* New York: Simon & Schuster, 1999. First published in 1974, this Newbery Award–winning book by an Ohio author tells the story of teenager M.C.'s efforts to deal with a spoil heap, full of waste from a strip mine, that is coming closer to his family's beloved home.

Sanders, Scott Russell. *Warm as Wool.* New York: Bradbury Press, 1998. In this picture book set in the early 1800s, a pioneer family in Ohio nearly freezes during the winter. The resourceful mother saves her money to buy some sheep to shear for wool.

Schulz, Walter A. *Will and Orv.* Minneapolis: Carolrhoda Books, Inc., 1991. Inventors Wilbur and Orville Wright came from Dayton, Ohio, to Kitty Hawk, North Carolina, to test their flying machine. This book describes what happened on the day of their first successful flight.

WEBSITES

State of Ohio Government Information and Services
<http://www.state.oh.us/>
Ohio's official website provides helpful facts about the state and
links to state agencies.

Ohio Tourism
<http://www.ohiotourism.com/>
The Ohio Division of Travel and Tourism offers information about
popular events and vacation destinations in Ohio.

The Columbus Dispatch
<http://www.dispatch.com/>
Catch up with current events in Ohio by reading the newspaper
from the state capital.

PRONUNCIATION GUIDE

Akron (AK-ruhn)

Cincinnati (sihn-suh-NAT-ee)

Cuyahoga (ky-uh-HOH-guh)

Iroquois (IHR-uh-kwoy)

Marietta (mar-ee-EHT-uh)

Maumee (maw-MEE)

Muskingum (muh-SKIHNG-uhm)

Sciota (sy-OHT-uh)

Shawnee (shaw-NEE)

Tuscarawas (tuhs-kuh-RAW-uhs)

Wyandot (WY-uhn-daht)

The Cincinnati skyline at night

GLOSSARY

colony: a territory ruled by a country some distance away

glacier: a large body of ice and snow that moves slowly over land

Great Lakes: a chain of five lakes in Canada and the northern United States. They are Lakes Superior, Michigan, Huron, Erie, and Ontario.

groundwater: water that lies beneath the earth's surface and supplies wells and springs. The water comes from rain and snow that seep through soil into cracks and other openings in rocks.

hazardous waste site: a collection point for used chemicals and other wastes that can harm living things or the environment

landfill: a place specially prepared for burying waste

leachate: liquid that has seeped through waste or that forms when waste rots in a landfill. Leachate can contaminate water or soil.

plateau: a large, relatively flat area that stands above the surrounding land

till: a mixture of clay, sand, and gravel dragged along by a glacier and left behind when the ice melts

toxic waste: a poisonous material that contaminates the environment and that can cause death, disease, or other defects

Underground Railroad: a system of escape routes that helped slaves get from the South to the North or Canada, where they would be free

INDEX

PHOTO ACKNOWLEDGMENTS

© W. Cody/ Corbis (cover left); © Bill Ross/ Corbis (cover right); © Lee Snider/ Corbis (title page left); © Jay Dickman/ Corbis (title page right); Digital Cartographics, pp. 1, 8, 9, 44; © Frank Lane Picture Agency/ Corbis, p. 4(detail), 7(detail), 18(detail), 38(detail), 51(detail); © James Blank/Root Resources, pp. 6, 12, 13, 52; ODNR, pp. 10, 14, 15, 26, 37, 43, 49, 56, 59; Kent and Donna Dannen, pp. 11, 19 (top); © Kohout Productions/Root Resources, p. 16; Maslowski Photo, p 17; The Cincinnati Historical Society, pp. 19 (bottom), 28; Michael J. Kabes, p. 20; Ohio Historical Society, pp. 21, 23, 24, 30, 34, 35, 61, 66 (second from top); Library of Congress, pp. 22, 27, 33, 66 (second from bottom); The Saint Louis Mercantile Library, p. 25; Cincinnati Art Museum, p. 29; The Western Reserve Historical Society, Cleveland, Ohio, p. 31, 68 (top, second from top); © Bettman/Corbis, p. 36; © Rod Berry, pp. 39, 80; Nesnadny & Schwartz, p. 40; © ALLSPORT USA / Tom Pigeon, p. 41; Cedar Point photo by Dan Feicht, p. 42; GE Aircraft Engines, Cincinnati, Ohio, p. 45; General Motors, p. 46; Ohio Apple Marketing Program, p. 47; Monica V. Brown, Photographic Artist, p. 48; © 1992 Daniel E. Dempster, p. 50; Hans-Olaf Pfannkuch, p. 54; Ohio Environmental Protection Agency, p. 55; Information & Applied Communications, Ohio State University, p. 57; S. Maslowski/Visuals Unlimited, p. 58; Lynn M. Stone, p. 60; Tim Seeley, pp. 63, 71, 72; The Ohioana Library, p. 66 (top); Hollywood Book and Poster, Inc., pp. 66 (bottom), 68 (bottom); Office of the Senator, p. 67 (top); Adam Stoltman, p. 67 (second from top); © Maria Mulas, p. 67 (second from the bottom); Circus World Museum, p. 67 (bottom); Cincinnati Reds, p. 68 (second from bottom); Joseph Marzullo, Retna Ltd., p. 69 (top); *Dictionary of American Potraits*, p. 69 (second from top); © David Allen/Corbis, p. 69 (second from bottom); Travel Information Division, Department of Conservation and Development, Raleigh, North Carolina, p. 69 (bottom); © Tom & Pat Leeson, p. 73; © David Muench/ Corbis, p. 75;

01/02